# Super Simple Ground Beef Cookbook

### The Easiest and Most Affordable Family Friendly Recipes

## BY

## MOLLY MILLS

# License Notes

# An Amazing Offer for Buying My Book!

Thank you very much for purchasing my books! As a token of my appreciation, I would like to extend an amazing offer to you! When you have subscribed with your e-mail address, you will have the opportunity to get free and discounted e-books that will show up in your inbox daily. You will also receive reminders before an offer expires so you never miss out. With just little effort on your part, you will have access to the newest and most informative books at your fingertips. This is all part of the VIP treatment when you subscribe below.

**SIGN ME UP:** *https://molly.gr8.com*

# Table of Contents

# Chapter I - Ground Beef Cooking Tips

When you first hear the term ground beef many of you will actually begin to think about hamburgers, meatballs, or even a meatloaf. With ground beef you can make a variety of different dishes without having to break your bank account. In this section I want to give you a few ground beef cooking tips so that you can make the most out of this versatile ingredient to make some of the tastiest dishes you will ever make.

AAAAAAAAAAAAAAAAAAAAAAAAAAAAAAAAAAAAAAAAAAAAAAAAAA

# (1) Never Cook Frozen Ground Beef

If you are going to cook ground beef, then you want to make sure that you do it the right way. The worst thing that you can do is actually cook frozen ground beef. There are many reasons for this but first and foremost being that the natural juice in your ground beef will turn into ice crystals, which when cooking will rinse off any of the flavor with your fat.

If you still want to retain the flavor of your ground beef, then I highly recommend thawing your ground beef in the refrigerator so that any frozen crystals can melt before you actually cook it.

ΛΛΛΛΛΛΛΛΛΛΛΛΛΛΛΛΛΛΛΛΛΛΛΛΛΛΛΛΛΛΛΛΛΛΛΛΛΛΛΛΛΛΛΛΛΛΛΛΛΛΛ

## (2) Reduce the Fat Content

If you were looking to be health conscious and want to reduce the amount of fat content that is in your ground beef, then I highly recommend rinsing your ground beef right after you cook it and brown it. All that you have to do is once your ground beef is fully brown in color, place it into a colander and then rinse it with some hot water. Then drain the water from your beef and blot dry with a few paper towels and set aside.

While this can certainly help to reduce the amount of fat content in your ground beef, you need to keep in mind that when you do this the flavor of your ground beef will also disappear.

AAAAAAAAAAAAAAAAAAAAAAAAAAAAAAAAAAAAAAAAAAAAAAAAA

# (3) Only Cook Your Ground Beef over Medium Heat

When it comes to cooking ground beef you want to keep in mind that the higher the temperature you cook it at, the higher the shrinkage rate will be. So for optimum results make sure that you cook your ground beef only at a medium temperature rather than at high temperature. If you cook your ground beef at a higher temperature you will risk making ground beef that is dry and tasteless.

AAAAAAAAAAAAAAAAAAAAAAAAAAAAAAAAAAAAAAAAAAAAAAAAAAAA

# (4) Always Use Fresh Ground Beef

While this may seem like common sense it is still something I want to bring up. If you are going to use ground beef in your recipes, it is best to always use fresh ground beef. Not only will this help to enhance the flavor of your dish, but it also can lead to healthier results in the long run.

# (5) Avoid Sticking

When you are cooking ground beef generally you will begin to use your hands to mix all of the ingredients together, especially when making hamburgers or meatballs. To avoid the meat sticking to your hands simply dip your hands in some cold water before you actually handle it. Also keep in mind that you do not want to over handle the meat, especially when you are making patties. Always just handle your meat with a very light touch and try not to compact it too much.

# (6) Never Use a Spatula

I know there are many of us that use spatulas when cooking hamburgers and that we often tend to press down the hamburger as it cooks. This is something I highly recommend not doing as this will actually cause your burgers to lose all their flavor and juices. Instead I highly recommend using a pair of tongs to turn over your burgers while they are cooking instead of a spatula.

AAAAAAAAAAAAAAAAAAAAAAAAAAAAAAAAAAAAAAAAAAAAAAAAA

# Chapter II - Delicious Ground Beef Recipes

AAAAAAAAAAAAAAAAAAAAAAAAAAAAAAAAAAAAAAAAAAAAAAAAAA

# Recipe 1: Easy Burrito Pie

Here is yet another Mexican inspired dish that I guarantee even the pickiest of eaters are going to fall in love with. This dish is very similar to lasagna and packed full of enough spice to last an entire lifetime.

**Yield:** 16 Servings

**Cooking Time:** 1 Hour

**List of Ingredients:**

- 2 Pounds of Beef, Ground and Lean
- 1 Onion, Large in Size and Finely Chopped
- 2 teaspoons of Garlic, Minced
- 1 Can of Black Olives, Finely Sliced
- 1 Can of Chili Peppers, Green in Color and Finely Diced
- 1 Can of Tomatoes with Green Chilies, Finely Diced
- 1 Jar of Taco Sauce
- 2 Cans of Beans, Refried Variety
- 12 Tortillas, Floured Variety
- 9 Ounces of Colby Cheese, Finely Shredded

AAA

**Instructions:**

1. The first thing you want to do is preheat your oven to 350 degrees.

2. While your oven is heating up use a large size skillet and cook your ground beef for at least five minutes.

3. Then add in your onion and garlic and cook for another 5 minutes. Remove from heat and drain excess liquid.

4. Next add in your next 6 ingredients and stir thoroughly to combine. Then reduce your heat to low and allow your mixture to simmer for at least 15 to 20 minutes.

5. Pour a very thin layer of your meat mixture into the bottom of a generously greased casserole dish. Cover with a layer of your tortillas followed by another layer of your meat then top with a layer of cheese. Repeat layers until all of your ingredients have been used.

6. Place into your oven to bake for the next 20 to 30 minutes or until your cheese is slightly brown in color. Remove and serve while still piping hot. Enjoy!

# Recipe 2: Cheeseburger Style Soup

Here is a filling soup recipe that you are going to want to make all of the time. It is a great dish to make on a cold winter night or whenever you are looking for something rather simplistic. Either way I know you are going to love it.

**Yield:** 8 Servings

**Cooking Time:** 50 Minutes

**List of Ingredients:**

- ½ Pound of Beef, Ground and Lean
- ¾ Cup of Onion, Large in Size and Finely Chopped
- ¾ Cup of Carrots, Fresh and Finely Shredded
- ¾ Cup of Celery, Fresh and Finely Diced
- 1 teaspoon of Basil, Dried
- 1 teaspoon of Parsley, Dried
- 4 Tablespoons of Butter, Soft
- 3 Cups of Broth, Chicken Variety and Homemade Preferable
- 4 Cups of Potatoes, Cut into Small Cubes
- ¼ Cup of Flour, All Purpose Variety
- 2 Cups of Cheddar Cheese, Cut into Small Cubes
- 1 ½ Cups of Milk, Whole
- ¼ Cup of Sour Cream

AAAAAAAAAAAAAAAAAAAAAAAAAAAAAAAAAAAAAAAAAAAAAAAAAAA

**Instructions:**

1. Use a large sized pot and melt your butter over medium heat. Add in your vegetables and beef and cook until your beef is thoroughly brown in color.

2. Next add in your next 4 ingredients and bring your mixture to a boil. Once the mixture is boiling reduce the heat with summer and allow your potatoes to cook until they are tender. This should take about 10 to 12 minutes.

3. Melt any remaining butter that you have and add in your next 3 ingredients, making sure to stir thoroughly until smooth in consistency.

4. Bring your soup to a boil and then reduce the heat to low. Add in your cheese and sour cream, making sure to stir thoroughly to combine. Continue cooking until completely heated through. Remove from heat and serve right away.

# Recipe 3: Sweet and Sour Meatballs

These meatballs are always a tasty treat to enjoy during the holiday season. After getting a taste of this dish I know this will soon become a favorite in your household.

**Yield:** 10 Servings

**Cooking Time:** 1 Hour

**List of Ingredients:**

- 1 Egg, Large in Size and Beaten
- ¼ Cup of Water, Warm
- 1 Pound of Beef, Ground
- 2 Slices of Bread, Crumbled
- Dash of Salt, For Taste
- Dash of Pepper, For Taste
- 1 Cup of Ketchup, Your Favorite Kind
- 1 Cup of Bouillon, Beef Variety
- ½ Cup of Vinegar
- ½ Cup of Brown Sugar, Light and packed
- 2 Tablespoons of Cornstarch

AAAAAAAAAAAAAAAAAAAAAAAAAAAAAAAAAAAAAAAAAAAAAAAAAA

**Instructions:**

1. The first thing you want to do is preheat your oven to 350 degrees.

2. Then take a small sized bowl and beat together your water and egg until thoroughly combined.

3. Then add in your next 4 ingredients and continue to stir until combined. Form your mixture into small sized meatballs and place them inside a large sized baking dish.

4. Place your meatballs into your oven to bake until they are brown in color. This should take at least 25 to 30 minutes.

5. While your meatballs are cooking combine your next three ingredients in a large size saucepan placed over medium heat. Add in your cornstarch and brown sugar and continue to stir until thick in consistency. Bring this mixture to a boil and then reduce the heat to low. Allow your mixture to cook for the next 5 minutes and remove from heat.

6. Pour this mixture over your meatballs and toss to combine. Serve when you are ready.

# Recipe 4: Tennessee Style Meatloaf

If you are looking for the best tasting meatloaf recipe out there, then this is the perfect recipe for you. While it does have a ton of ingredients that you will be using, don't be fooled. This is actually a very easy meatloaf dish to make.

**Yield:** 10 Servings

**Cooking Time:** 1 Hour and 55 Minutes

**Ingredients for Your Brown Sugar Glaze:**

- ½ Cup of Ketchup, Your Favorite Kind
- ¼ Cup of Brown Sugar, Light and Packed
- 2 Tablespoons of Vinegar, Cider Variety

**Ingredients for Your Meatloaf:**

- Some Cooking Spray
- 1 Onion, Large in Size and Finely Chopped
- ½ A Green Bell Pepper, Finely Chopped
- 2 Cloves of Garlic, Minced
- 2 Eggs, Large in Size and Beaten
- 1 teaspoon of Thyme, Dried
- 1 teaspoon of Salt, For Taste
- ½ teaspoons of Black Pepper, For Taste
- 2 teaspoons of Mustard
- 2 teaspoons of Worcestershire Sauce
- ½ teaspoons of Tabasco
- ½ Cup of Milk, Whole
- 2/3 Cup of Oats, Quick Cooking variety
- 1 Pound of Beef, Lean and Ground
- ½ Pound of Pork, Ground
- ½ Pound of Veal, Ground

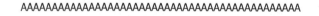

AAAAAAAAAAAAAAAAAAAAAAAAAAAAAAAAAAAAAAAAAAAAAAAAA

**Instructions:**

1. The first thing you want to do this combine your first 3 ingredients into a medium sized bowl, stirring well until next.

2. Then preheat your oven to 350 degrees. While your oven is heating up spray two loaf pans with a generous amount of cooking spray in line with some aluminum foil.

3. Place your green peppers and onions in a microwave safe container and cook until soft. This should take about 1 to 2 minutes. Set aside for later use.

4. Then use a large sized mixing bowl and combine your next 10 ingredients together, making sure to stir well to combine. Then add in your cooked onions and green peppers, stirring well to combine.

5. Add in your next three ingredients and using your hands work well until thoroughly mixed together.

6. Divide up your meatloaf mixture into your 2 loaf pans and brush with a bit of your premade glaze.

7. Place into your oven to bake for the next 50 minutes. After this time remove and brush with your remaining glaze. Return back to your oven and continue cooking for the next 10 minutes. Remove from oven and allow to sit for 15 minutes before serving. Enjoy.

# Recipe 5: Chipotle Style Lasagna

If you don't like lasagna, it doesn't mean that you can't enjoy a lasagna dish that you will fall in love with in the future. This is a low carb dish that you will love to enjoy if you are looking for something a little healthier.

**Yield:** 12 Servings

**Cooking Time:** 2 Hours

**List of Ingredients:**

- 1 Pound of Beef, Ground and Lean
- 1 Pound of Sausage, Italian Variety and Hot
- 1 Onion, Large in Size and Finely Chopped
- 1 Pint of Mushrooms, Fresh and Finely Sliced
- 3 Cloves of Garlic, Minced
- 1 Chile, Chipotle Variety in Adobo Sauce and Finely Chopped
- 1 Can of Tomato Paste
- 2 Cans of Tomatoes, Stewed Variety
- Dash of Sea Salt, For Taste
- Dash of Black Pepper, For Taste
- ½ Cup of Basil, Fresh and Roughly Chopped

- ¼ Cup of Oregano, Fresh and Roughly Chopped
- 2 Packs of Cream Cheese, Warmed to Room Temperature
- 1 Pound of Spinach, Frozen, Thawed and Roughly Chopped
- 9 Noodles, Lasagna Variety
- 2 Balls of Mozzarella, Fresh and Finely Sliced
- 2 Zucchini, Fresh and Sliced Thinly
- 1 Cup of Cheese, Asiago Variety and Finely Grated
- 1 Cup of Cheese, Parmesan Variety and Finely Grated

AAAAAAAAAAAAAAAAAAAAAAAAAAAAAAAAAAAAAAAAAAAAAAAAA

**Instructions:**

1. The first thing you want to do is cook your ground beef and sausage together in a large sized pan placed over medium to high heat. Cook until light brown and color. Remove and drain any excess grease before stirring in your next three ingredients.

2. Continue to cook until your onions are soft and then add in your next three ingredients. Stir to combine.

3. Bring this mixture to a simmer and allowed to cook for the next 15 minutes. Season with a dash of salt and pepper and then add in your basil and oregano. Continue cooking for another 5 minutes and then remove from heat.

4. While your sauce is cooking stir together your spinach and cream cheese in a separate size bowl until thoroughly blended. Set aside.

5. Then preheat your oven to 400 degrees. While your oven is heating up line the bottom of a medium sized baking dish with some aluminum foil and grease it lightly with some cooking spray.

6. Place your lasagna noodles into the bottom of your pan and spread in some of your cream cheese mixture on top. Top with your meat sauce and then layer your cheese and zucchini. Repeat layers until all of your ingredients have been used up.

7. Cover your baking dish with aluminum foil and place into your oven to bake for the next 40 minutes. After this time remove the aluminum foil and continue to bake for the next 15 to 20 minutes or until the top is light brown in color. Remove and serve right away. Enjoy.

# Recipe 6: Easy Sloppy Joes

If you are a huge fan of sloppy joes, then you need to try this recipe out for yourself. This is a great recipe to put together if you want to save yourself sometime in the kitchen.

**Yield:** 6 Servings

**Cooking Time:** 40 Minutes

**List of Ingredients:**

- 1 Pound of Beef, Ground and Lean
- ¼ Cup of Onion, Large in Size and Finely Chopped
- ¼ Cup of Green Bell Pepper, Finely Chopped
- ½ teaspoons of Garlic, Powdered
- 1 teaspoon of Yellow Mustard, Prepared
- ¾ Cup of Ketchup, Your Favorite Kind
- 3 teaspoons of Brown Sugar, Light and Packed
- Dash of Salt, For Taste
- Dash of Black Pepper, For Taste

AAAAAAAAAAAAAAAAAAAAAAAAAAAAAAAAAAAAAAAAAAAAAAAAAA

**Instructions:**

1. Use a medium sized skillet placed over medium heat and add in your ground beef, onions and peppers. Cook until your beef is brown in color. Remove and drain the excess liquid.

2. Add in your remaining ingredients and allow your dish to simmer for at least 30 minutes. Season with some salt and pepper and then remove from heat. Serve whenever you are ready.

# Recipe 7: The Poor Man's Classic Stroganoff

This is the perfect recipe for those who are on a tight budget and still need to feed a large group of people. With this dish you never have to worry about feeding your friends and family by breaking your bank account in the process.

**Yield:** 4 Servings

**Cooking Time:** 30 Minutes

**List of Ingredients:**

- 1 Pack of Noodles, Egg Variety
- 1 Pound of Beef, Ground and Lean
- 1 teaspoon of Greek Style Seasoning
- Dash of Salt, For Taste
- Dash of Pepper, For Taste
- 1 teaspoon of Oil, Vegetable Variety
- 1 Pack of Mushrooms, Fresh and Finely Sliced
- 1 Pint of Sour Cream

AAAAAAAAAAAAAAAAAAAAAAAAAAAAAAAAAAAAAAAAAAAAAAAAAAAA

**Instructions:**

1. The first thing you want to do is bring a large size pot of water to a boil and season with some salt. Add in your noodles and cook until they are tender. This should take about 5 minutes. Remove, drain and set aside.

2. Then heat up a large sized skillet placed over medium to high heat. Add in your ground beef and cook until brown in color. This should take about 5 to 7 minutes. Remove, drain and get rid of the excess grease. Season with your salt, pepper and Greek seasoning.

3. Next heat up some oil in a large sized skillet place over medium heat. Add in your mushrooms and cook just until they are tender. This take about 5 minutes. Remove and add to your ground beef.

4. Stir together your cream cheese and ground beef mixture and cook until piping hot. This take about 5 minutes. Remove and serve over a bed of egg noodles and enjoy.

# Recipe 8: Tasty Baked Ziti

Here is an Italian style inspired recipe that I know you are going to fall in love with. Feel free to make this dish without meat if you wish.

**Yield:** 10 Servings

**Cooking Time:** 55 Minutes

**List of Ingredients:**

- 1 Pound of Pasta, Ziti Variety and Dry
- 1 Onion, Large in Size and Finely Chopped
- 1 Pound of Beef, Lean and Ground
- 2 Jars of Spaghetti Sauce, Your Favorite Kind
- 6 Ounces of Provolone Style Cheese, Finely Sliced
- 1 ½ Cups of Sour Cream
- 6 Ounces of Mozzarella Cheese, Finely Shredded
- 2 Tablespoons of Parmesan Cheese, Finely Grated

AAAAAAAAAAAAAAAAAAAAAAAAAAAAAAAAAAAAAAAAAAAAAAAAAAA

**Instructions:**

1. The first thing you want to do is cook your pasta. To do this bring a large size pot of water to a boil and then add in your pasta. Cook until tender. This should take about 8 minutes. After this time remove and drain. Set aside for later use.

2. While your pasta is cooking use a large sized skillet and brown together your ground beef and onion over medium heat.

3. Once your beef is brown add in your spaghetti sauce and allow to cook for the next 15 minutes over a simmer.

4. Preheat your oven to 350 degrees. While your oven is heating up grease a medium sized baking dish with a generous amount of cooking spray.

5. Add in your ingredients in layers starting with: half of your cooked pasta, your provolone cheese, some sour cream, half of your sauce mix, and repeat the layers. Top with your Parmesan cheese.

6. Place into your oven to bake for the next 30 minutes or until your cheese is completely melted. Remove and allow to cool slightly before serving.

# Recipe 9: Hot Tamale Style Pie

This is a great pie style recipe to make if you are looking to bring some authentic Mexican taste to your kitchen. Once you make this dish I know you are going to fall in love with it.

**Yield:** 8 Servings

**Cooking Time:** 1 Hour and 30 Minutes

**List of Ingredients:**

- Some Cooking Spray
- 2 Pounds of Beef, Lean and Ground
- 2 Cups of Peppers, Poblano Style and Finely Diced
- 1 teaspoon of Salt, For Taste
- 1 Jar of Salsa, Your Favorite Kind
- ½ teaspoons of Oregano, Dried
- 1 teaspoon of Pepper, Chipotle Variety, Ground and Dried
- 2 Boxes of Corn Muffin Mix, Dried
- 2 Eggs, Large in Size and Beaten
- 2/3 Cup of Milk, Whole and Evenly Divided
- 4 Ounces of Cheddar Cheese, Finely Shredded and Evenly Divided
- 4 Ounces of Monterey Jack Cheese, Finely Shredded and Evenly Divided
- 8 Ounces of Corn, Frozen and Thawed

AAAAAAAAAAAAAAAAAAAAAAAAAAAAAAAAAAAAAAAAAAAAAAAAAA

## Instructions:

1. The first thing you want to do is preheat your oven to 350 degrees. While your oven is heating up take a large size casserole dish and grease it with a generous amount of cooking spray.

2. Next cook your ground beef over medium to high heat in a large size saucepan for the next 5 minutes or until brown in color.

3. Reduce your heat to simmer and add in your next 5 ingredients, stirring well to combine. Cook for the next 10 minutes.

4. While your mixture is cooking mix together your corn muffin mix with your egg and milk in a large sized bowl. Whisk until thoroughly combined.

5. Then use a separate large sized bowl and mix together your other corn muffin mix with your egg, milk and cheese. Stir to thoroughly combine.

6. Spread mix without cheese into your baking dish and top with your other corn mix. Top with your cooked beef mixture.

# Recipe 10: Tailgate Style Chili

If you are looking for something a little heartier and incredibly filling, this is the perfect chili dish for you. This is the perfect dish that you can make the night before if you are tight on time.

**Yield:** 12 Servings

**Cooking Time:** 2 Hours and 30 Minutes

## List of Ingredients:

- 2 Pounds of Beef Chuck, Ground and Lean
- 1 Pound of Sausage, Italian Variety
- 3 Cans of Chili Beans, Drained
- 1 Can of Chili Beans, Placed in Spicy Sauce
- 2 Cans of Tomatoes, With Juice and Finely Diced
- 1 Can of Tomato Paste
- 1 Onion, Yellow in Color, Large in Size and Finely Chopped
- 3 Stalks of Celery, Finely Chopped
- 1 Green Bell Pepper, Seeded and Finely Chopped
- 1 Red Bell Pepper, Seeded and Finely Chopped
- 1 tablespoon of Bacon Bits
- 4 Cubes of Bouillon, Beef Variety
- ½ Cup of Beer, Your Favorite Kind and Dark Preferable
- ¼ Cup of Chili Powder
- 1 tablespoon of Worcestershire Sauce
- 1 tablespoon of Garlic, Minced
- 1 tablespoon of Oregano, Ground
- 2 teaspoons of Tabasco
- 1 teaspoon of Basil, Dried
- 1 teaspoon of Salt, For Taste

- 1 teaspoon of Black Pepper, For Taste
- 1 teaspoon of Cayenne Style Pepper
- 1 teaspoon of Paprika
- 1 teaspoon of Sugar, White
- 1 Bag of Fritos, Small in Size
- 1 Pack of Cheddar Cheese, Finely Shredded

**Instructions:**

1. First heat up a large sized stock pot over medium to high heat. Add in your ground chuck and sausage and cook until brown and color. Remove and drain the excess grease.

2. Add in your remaining ingredients except for your cheese and stir to thoroughly combine. Cook over a simmer for the next 2 hours, making sure to stir once in a while.

3. After this time season with some more seasonings if you wish and then remove from heat.

4. Ladle into serving bowls and top with corn chips and cheddar cheese. Enjoy while still piping hot.

# Recipe 11: Classic Stuffed Peppers

Surprisingly this dish has roots planted as far back as the Great Depression and even back then this dish was considered a delicious treat to enjoy. That being said this dish is a delicious one to enjoy if you are on a budget as you don't need a ton of ingredients to make it.

**Yield:** 8 Servings

**Cooking Time:** 1 Hour and 50 Minutes

**List of Ingredients:**

- 1 Cup of Rice, White in Color and Uncooked Variety
- 2 Cups of Water, Warm
- 1 Onion, Large in Size and Finely Diced
- 1 tablespoon of Olive Oil, Extra Virgin Variety
- 2 Cups of Marinara Sauce, Your Favorite Kind
- 1 Cup of Broth, Beef Variety
- ¼ teaspoons of Red Pepper Flakes, Crushed
- 1 Pound of Beef, Ground and Lean
- ¼ Pound of Sausage, Pork and Italian Variety and with Casings Removed
- 1 Can of Tomatoes, Finely Diced

- ¼ Cup of Parsley, Italian Variety, Fresh and Roughly Chopped
- 2 teaspoons of Salt, For Taste
- 1 teaspoon of Black Pepper, For Taste
- Dash of Cayenne Style Pepper
- 4 Green Bell Peppers, Large in Size, cut into Halves and Seeded
- 1 Cup of Cheese, parmigiana-Reggiano Variety and Finely Grated

AAAAAAAAAAAAAAAAAAAAAAAAAAAAAAAAAAAAAAAAAAAAAAAAAA

**Instructions:**

1. The first thing you want to do is preheat your oven to 375 degrees.

2. Then bring your rice and water to a boil in a medium sized saucepan placed over medium heat. Once boiling reduce the heat to low and continue to cook your rice until the liquid has been fully absorbed. This should take about 20 to 25 minutes. Once thoroughly cooked remove from heat and satisfied.

3. While your rice is cooking cook your onion and olive oil together in a medium sized saucepan placed over medium heat. Cook until the onion is soft, about 5 minutes. Remove from heat and transfer your onion to a large sized bowl. Set aside.

4. Then add in your next 4 ingredients into a large sized skillet and cook for the next minute. Pour this sauce into a generously greased baking dish and set aside.

5. Next use a large sized bowl and combine your next 8 ingredients until thoroughly combined. Stir in your cooked rice and your cheese and stir again to combine.

6. Stuff your peppers with this mixture and place into your baking dish. Top with your tomato sauce and sprinkle with remaining cheese. Cover with aluminum foil.

7. Place into your oven to bake for the next 45 minutes. After this time remove the aluminum foil and continue cooking for the next 20 to 25 minutes or until your cheese is brown on the top and your peppers are tender to the touch. Remove and serve while still piping hot.

# Recipe 12: Beef Packed Spaghetti Squash

If you are looking for a healthy dish for the entire family to enjoy, then this is the perfect recipe for you. It is a delicious casserole that you can make when you are feeding a large group of people. I guarantee that after they have their first bite that they all will fall in love with it.

**Yield:** 6 Servings

**Cooking Time:** 1 Hour and 50 Minutes

**List of Ingredients:**

- 1 Spaghetti Style Squash, cut into Halves and Seeded
- 1 Pound of Beef, Ground and Lean
- ½ Cup of Green Bell Pepper, Finely Diced
- ½ Cup of Red Bell Pepper, Finely Diced
- ¼ Cup of Onion, Red in Color and Finely Diced
- 1 Clove of Garlic, Minced
- 1 Can of Tomatoes, Italian Style, Finely Diced and Undrained
- ½ teaspoons of Oregano, Dried
- ½ teaspoons of Basil, Dried
- ¼ teaspoons of Salt, For Taste
- ¼ teaspoons of Black Pepper, For Taste
- 2 ¼ Cups of Cheddar Cheese, Sharp Variety and Finely Shredded

ΛΛΛΛΛΛΛΛΛΛΛΛΛΛΛΛΛΛΛΛΛΛΛΛΛΛΛΛΛΛΛΛΛΛΛΛΛΛΛΛΛΛΛΛΛΛΛΛΛΛΛΛ

**Instructions:**

1. The first thing you want to do is preheat your oven to 375 degrees.

2. Then place your squash onto a large size baking sheet and bake for the next 40 minutes or until completely tender. Remove from the oven and shred using two forks.

3. Reduce your heat to 350 degrees. While your oven is lowering its heat grease a casserole dish with a generous amount of cooking spray.

4. Using a medium sized skillet placed over medium heat Cook your ground beef until it is brown in color. Remove and drain the excess grease

5. Add in your next 4 ingredients and continue to cook until your vegetables are nice and tender.

6. Mix in your remaining ingredients into your beef mixture except for your cheese until thoroughly combined. Continue cooking until completely heated through and then transfer to your casserole dish. Top with your shredded cheese.

7. Bake for the next 25 to 30 minutes or until your cheese is completely melted. Remove and serve right away.

# Recipe 13: Pizza Style Casserole

If you are a huge fan of pizza, then you need to try this dish out for yourself. This is a casserole dish that combines all of the ingredients and flavors of pizza in an easy to make dish that the entire family will fall in love with.

**Yield:** 7 Servings

**Cooking Time:** 1 Hour

**List of Ingredients:**

- 2 Cups of Noodles, Egg Variety and Uncooked
- ½ Pound of Beef, Ground and Lean
- 1 Onion, Large in Size and Finely Chopped
- 2 Cloves of Garlic, Minced
- 1 Green Bell Pepper, Finely Chopped
- 1 Cup of Sausage, Pepperoni Style and Finely Sliced
- 16 Ounces of Pizza Sauce, Your Favorite Kind
- 4 Tablespoons of Milk, Whole
- 1 Cup of Mozzarella Cheese, Finely Shredded

AAAAAAAAAAAAAAAAAAAAAAAAAAAAAAAAAAAAAAAAAAAAAAAAAAA

**Instructions:**

1. The first cook your noodles according to the directions on the package.

2. Then preheat your oven to 350 degrees.

3. Next use a medium sized skillet placed over medium to high heat and add in your ground beef with your next three ingredients. Cook until your ground beef is brown in color. Drain some of the excess fat and then add in your remaining ingredients except for your cheese. Stir well to combine.

4. Pour mixture into a generously greased casserole dish and bake for the next 20 minutes. After this time remove from your oven and top off with your cheese. Return back to your oven and continue cooking for the next 5 to 10 minutes or until your cheese is fully melted. Remove and allow to cool slightly before serving.

# Recipe 14: Brown Sugar Smothered Meatloaf

Here is yet another great tasting meatloaf recipe that I know your entire family will be drooling over. It is easy to make and tastes just as great as it smells.

**Yield:** 8 Servings

**Cooking Time:** 1 Hour and 30 Minutes

**List of Ingredients:**

- ½ Cup of Brown Sugar, Light and Packed
- ½ Cup of Ketchup, Your Favorite Kind
- 1 ½ Pounds of Beef, Ground and Lean
- ¾ Cup of Milk, Whole
- 2 Eggs, Large in Size and Beaten
- 1 ½ teaspoons of Salt, For Taste
- ¼ teaspoons of Black Pepper, For Taste
- 1 Onion, Small in Size and Finely Chopped
- ¼ teaspoons of Ginger, Ground
- ¾ Cup of Saltine Crackers, Crushed Finely

AAAAAAAAAAAAAAAAAAAAAAAAAAAAAAAAAAAAAAAAAAAAAAAAAA

**Instructions:**

1. The first thing you want to do is preheat your oven to 350 degrees. While your oven is heating up grease a medium sized loaf pan with some cooking spray.

2. Press your brown sugar into the bottom of your greased loaf pan and spread your ketchup over the top.

3. Then use a large size to mixing bowl and mixed together your remaining ingredients. Use your hands and shape your mixture into a loaf and place it on top of your ketchup in your loaf pan.

4. Place into your oven to bake for at least one hour. After this time remove and allow to cool slightly before serving.

# Recipe 15: Miniature Meatloaves

Here is another easy to make recipe that the entire family will enjoy. The ketchup and light brown sugar that you will be using in this dish helps to give it a tangy and sweet flavor that you won't be able to resist.

**Yield:** 8 Servings

**Cooking Time:** 1 Hour

**List of Ingredients:**

- 1 Egg, Large in Size and Beaten
- ¾ Cup of Milk, Whole
- 1 Cup of Cheddar Cheese, Finely Shredded
- ½ Cup of Oats, Quick Cooking Variety
- 1 teaspoon of Salt, For Taste
- 1 Pound of Beef, Ground and Lean
- 2/3 Cup of Ketchup, Your Favorite Kind
- ¼ Cup of Brown Sugar, Light and Packed
- 1 ½ teaspoons of Mustard, Prepared Variety

AAAAAAAAAAAAAAAAAAAAAAAAAAAAAAAAAAAAAAAAAAAAAAAAAAAA

**Instructions:**

1. The first thing you want to do is preheat your oven to 350 degrees.

2. While your oven is heating up use a large sized bowl and combine your first five ingredients together. Stir thoroughly combined.

3. Then add in your ground beef, using your hands to make an evenly mixed mixture. Form your mix into a small sized meatloaves and place into a lightly greased baking dish.

4. Next using a separate small sized bowl combine your next three ingredients, making sure to stir thoroughly to combine. Pour this mixture over your meatloaves.

5. Place into your oven to bake for the next 45 minutes. After this time remove from oven and allow to cool slightly before serving.

# Recipe 16: Best Hamburger Patties Ever

If you are looking to make hamburgers during your next family get together. These are the best burgers to make during the summer time and can be paired alongside some healthy coleslaw or a summer salad.

**Yield:** 4 Servings

**Cooking Time:** 30 Minutes

**List of Ingredients:**

- 1 ½ Pound of Beef, Ground and Lean
- ½ of an Onion, Large in Size and Finely Chopped
- ½ Cup of Cheddar Cheese, Finely Shredded
- 1 teaspoon of Soy Sauce, Low in Salt
- 1 teaspoon of Worcestershire Sauce
- 1 Egg, Large in Size and Beaten Lightly
- 1 Pack of Onion Soup Mix, Dry
- 1 Clove of Garlic, Minced
- 1 tablespoon of Garlic, Powdered
- 1 teaspoon of Parsley, Dried
- 1 teaspoon of Basil, Dried
- 1 teaspoon of Oregano, Dried
- ½ teaspoons of Rosemary, Dried and Crushed
- Dash of Salt, For Taste
- Dash of Pepper, For Taste

AAAAAAAAAAAAAAAAAAAAAAAAAAAAAAAAAAAAAAAAAAAAAAAAA

**Instructions:**

1. The first thing you want to do is preheat your grill to high heat.

2. Then use a large sized mixing bowl and mix together your first 15 ingredients together. Using your hands mix well until thoroughly combined.

3. Then form your mixture into 4 equal sized patties.

4. Place the patties on your grill and grill for at least 5 minutes per side or until done to your liking. Serve on hamburger buns and with your favorite condiments. Enjoy right away.

# Recipe 17: Asian Style Lettuce Wraps

If you are looking for a healthy and great tasting dinner dish, then this is the perfect recipe for you. This is a great dish to make when you want to entertain a large group of people and leave them craving your food.

**Yield:** 4 Servings

**Cooking Time:** 35 Minutes

## List of Ingredients:

- 16 Lettuce Leaves, Butter Variety
- 1 Pound of Beef, Ground and Lean
- 1 tablespoon of Oil, Cooking Variety
- 1 Onion, Large in Size and Finely Chopped
- ¼ Cup of Hoisin Sauce
- 2 Cloves of Garlic, Fresh and Minced
- 1 tablespoon of Soy Sauce, Low in Sodium
- 1 tablespoon of Vinegar, Rice Wine Variety
- 2 teaspoons of Ginger, Pickled and Minced
- Dash of Pepper Sauce, Chile and Asian Variety
- 1 Can of Chestnuts, Water Variety, Drained and Finely Chopped
- 1 Bunch of Onions, Green in Color and Finely Chopped
- 2 teaspoons of Oil, Sesame Variety and Dark in Color

AAAAAAAAAAAAAAAAAAAAAAAAAAAAAAAAAAAAAAAAAAAAAAAAAA

**Instructions:**

1. First rinse your lettuce leaves and pat dry with a paper towel. Set aside.

2. Then use a large sized skillet police over medium to high heat and cook up your ground beef in some oil until light brown in color. They should take about 5 to 7 minutes. Drain the excess grease and transfer your beef into a large sized bowl.

3. Using the same skillet cook your onions for the next 5 to 10 minutes or until nice and tender. Then add in your next 6 ingredients and stir to combine.

4. Add in your remaining ingredients including your cooked beef and cook just until your onions begin to wilt. Just take about 2 minutes.

5. Pile your ground beef mixture into the center of your lettuce leaves and roll burrito style. Continue until all of your meat mixture has been used up. Serve right away and enjoy.

# Recipe 18: Beef and Bean Packed Chimichangas

Here is yet another great tasting Mexican dish that I know you won't be able to resist for long. The best part about this dish is that it is incredibly healthy considering that this dish is baked instead of fried. It is healthy and incredibly delicious.

**Yield:** 8 Servings

**Cooking Time:** 45 Minutes

**List of Ingredients:**

- 1 Pound of Beef, Ground and Lean
- ¾ Cup of Onion, Large in Size and Finely Chopped
- ¾ Cup of Green Bell Peppers, Finely Diced
- 1 ½ Cups of Corn, Whole Kernel Variety
- 2 Cups of Taco Sauce
- 2 teaspoons of Chili, Powdered Variety
- 1 teaspoon of Salt, Garlic Variety
- 1 teaspoon of Cumin, Ground
- 1 Can of Beans, Refried Variety
- 8 Tortillas, Floured Variety
- 1 Pack of Monterey Style Cheese, Finely Shredded
- 1 tablespoon of Butter, Fully Melted
- Some Lettuce, Finely Shredded
- 1 Tomato, Fresh and Finely Diced

AAAAAAAAAAAAAAAAAAAAAAAAAAAAAAAAAAAAAAAAAAAAAAAAAA

**Instructions:**

1. The first thing you want to do is preheat your oven to 350 degrees.

2. Then cook your ground beef in a medium sized skillet placed over medium to high heat until brown in color. Remove and drain the excess grease. Return to heat.

3. Next add in your next 3 ingredients and cook for at least 5 more minutes or until your vegetables are nice and tender.

4. Add in your remaining ingredients except for your cheese and stir thoroughly combine.

5. Spoon this mixture into your tortillas and wrap them up burrito style. Place them into a medium sized baking dish and brush with some melted butter. Top with your shredded cheese.

6. Place into your oven to bake for the next 30 to 35 minutes or until golden brown in color. Remove and serve whenever you are ready.

# Recipe 19: Cocktail Style Meatballs

Once you serve these meatballs at your next party, be prepared for them to disappear as quickly as you serve them. These make the perfect appetizers to serve for your next Christmas or New Year's Eve party.

**Yield:** 10 Servings

**Cooking Time:** 1 Hour and 45 Minutes

**List of Ingredients:**

- 1 Pound of Beef, Ground and Lean
- 1 Egg, Large in Size and Beaten
- 2 Tablespoons of Water, Warm
- ½ Cup of Bread Crumbs
- 3 Tablespoons of Onion, Minced
- 1 Can of Cranberry Sauce, Jellied Variety
- ¾ Cup of Chili Sauce
- 1 tablespoon of Brown Sugar, Light and Packed
- 1 ½ teaspoons of Lemon Juice, Fresh

∧∧∧∧∧∧∧∧∧∧∧∧∧∧∧∧∧∧∧∧∧∧∧∧∧∧∧∧∧∧∧∧∧∧∧∧∧∧∧∧∧∧∧∧∧∧

**Instructions:**

1. First preheat your oven to 350 degrees.

2. While your oven is heating up use a large sized bowl and combine your first 4 ingredients together until evenly mixed. Roll this mixture into small sized meatballs and place into a generously greased baking dish.

3. Place into your oven to bake for the next 20 to 25 minutes, making sure to only turn the meatballs once.

4. Then use a large size saucepan and combine your remaining ingredients together until evenly mixed.

5. Add in your cooked meatballs to your sauce and allow to simmer for the next hour before you serve.

# Recipe 20: Easy Wet Style Burritos

Here is yet another delicious Mexican inspired recipe that I know you won't be able to resist. For the tastiest results I highly recommend serving this dish with some of your favorite type of salsa and some sour cream to make it truly delicious.

**Yield:** 6 Servings

**Cooking Time:** 45 Minutes

**List of Ingredients:**

- 1 Pound of Beef, Ground and Lean
- ½ Cup of Onion, Large in Size and Finely Chopped
- 1 Clove of Garlic, Minced
- ½ teaspoons of Cumin
- ¼ teaspoons of Salt, For Taste
- 1/8 teaspoons of Pepper, For Taste
- 1 Can of Green Chile Peppers, Finely Diced
- 1 Can of Beans, Refried Variety
- 1 Can of Chili, Without Beans Preferable
- 1 Can of Tomato Soup, Condensed
- 1 Can of Enchilada Style Sauce
- 6 Tortillas, Four Variety and Warmed Slightly
- 2 Cups of Lettuce, Finely Shredded
- 1 Cup of Tomatoes, Finely Chopped
- 2 Cups of Cheese, Mexican Blend and Finely Shredded
- ½ Cup of Onions, Green in Color and Finely Chopped

AAAAAAAAAAAAAAAAAAAAAAAAAAAAAAAAAAAAAAAAAAAAAAAAAAAA

**Instructions:**

1. The first thing you want to do is cook ground beef in a medium sized skillet placed over medium to high heat. Cook until your beef is brown in color and then drain the excess grease. Season with your next 4 ingredients.

2. Then add in your next two ingredients and stir until well blended. Remove from heat and set aside.

3. Use a large sized saucepan and combine your next three ingredients together until evenly mixed. Cook over medium heat until completely heated through. Remove from heat and set aside.

4. Then set out your tortillas and spoon a spoonful of your ground beef mixture right into the center. Top with your favorite toppings and roll up tortilla style.

5. Place your tortilla on a microwave-safe plate and sprinkle cheese over the top. Microwave for at least 30 seconds or until your cheese is completely melted. Repeat until all of your ingredients have been used up. Serve whenever you are ready.

# Recipe 21: Slow Cooker Style Taco Soup

This is a quick and great tasting recipe that you can make if you are craving some authentic Mexican food. I guarantee that once they get a taste of it will fall in love with it, even the pickiest eaters. Feel free to adjust the amount of spice you add to this dish.

**Yield:** 8 Servings

**Cooking Time:** 8 Hours and 10 Minutes

## List of Ingredients:

- 1 Pound of Beef, Ground and Lean
- 1 Onion, Large in Size and Finely Chopped
- 1 Can of Chili Beans, With Liquid
- 1 Can of Kidney Beans, With Liquid
- 1 Can of Corn, Whole Kernel Variety and with Liquid
- 1 Can of Tomato Sauce
- 2 Cups of Water, Warm
- 2 Cans of Tomatoes, Peeled and Finely Diced
- 1 Can of Green Chile Peppers, Finely Diced
- 1 Pack of Taco Seasoning Mix, Your Favorite Kind

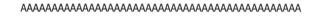

**Instructions:**

1. Using a large sized skillet placed over medium to high heat cook your ground beef until thoroughly brown in color. Once browned drain the excess grease and set aside.

2. Then place all of your ingredients into a slow cooker and stir well to combine.

3. Cook on the lowest setting for the next 8 hours. After this time feel free to serve your dish whenever you are ready.

# Recipe 22: Healthy Cabbage Roll Casserole

With the help of the last recipe that I gave you, now you can make this delicious casserole dish that is so tasty the entire family will want you to make over and over again.

**Yield:** 12 Servings

**Cooking Time:** 1 Hour and 40 Minutes

**List of Ingredients:**

- 2 Pounds of Beef, Ground and Lean
- 1 Cup of Onion, Large in Size and Finely Chopped
- 1 Can of Tomato Sauce
- 3 ½ Pounds of Cabbage, Roughly Chopped
- 1 Cup of Rice, White in Color and Uncooked
- 1 teaspoon of Salt, For Taste
- 2 Cans of Beef Broth, Homemade Preferable

AAAAAAAAAAAAAAAAAAAAAAAAAAAAAAAAAAAAAAAAAAAAAAAAAAAAA

**Instructions:**

1. The first thing you want to do is preheat your oven to 350 degrees.

2. While your oven is heating up use a large sized skillet and brown your beef over medium to high heat until your beef is brown and color. Once browned remove and drain the excess grease.

3. Next use a large sized mixing bowl and combine your next five ingredients together until evenly mixed. Toss in and your cooked beef and mix again to combine.

4. Pour this mixture into a generously greased baking dish and pour your broth over the top.

5. Place into your oven to bake for the next hour and 30 minutes. After this time remove and serve when you are ready.

# Recipe 23: Delicious Cabbage Rolls

These cabbage rolls make for a delicious and healthy meal that you will want to make over and over again. These rolls are smothered in a sweet and tangy sauce that you will fall in love with.

**Yield:** 6 Servings

**Cooking Time:** 9 Hours and 30 Minutes

**List of Ingredients:**

- 12 Cabbage Leaves, Fresh
- 1 Cup of Rice, Fully Cooked and White in Color
- 1 Egg, Large in Size and Lightly Beaten
- ¼ Cup of Milk, Whole
- ¼ Cup of Onion, Minced
- 1 Pound of Beef, Ground and Lean
- 1 ¼ teaspoons of Salt, For Taste
- 1 ¼ teaspoons of Pepper, For Taste
- 1 Can of Tomato Sauce, Small in Size
- 1 tablespoon of Brown Sugar, Light and Packed
- 1 tablespoon of Lemon Juice, Fresh
- 1 teaspoon of Worcestershire Sauce

AA

**Instructions:**

1. The first thing you want to do is bring a large sized pot of water to a boil. Once the water is boiling add in your cabbage leaves and allow to boil for at least 2 minutes. After the time remove and drain.

2. Then use a large sized bowl and combine your next 7 ingredients together until evenly combined. Take at least ¼ cup of this mixture and place it into the center of each cabbage leaf. Roll a burrito style and place into your slow cooker.

3. Next use a small sized bowl and mix together your remaining ingredients to make your sauce. Pour this mixture over your cabbage rolls.

4. Cover and cook on the lowest setting for the next eight to nine hours. After this time turn off your slow cooker and serve whenever you are ready.

# About the Author

Molly Mills always knew she wanted to feed people delicious food for a living. Being the oldest child with three younger brothers, Molly learned to prepare meals at an early age to help out her busy parents. She just seemed to know what spice went with which meat and how to make sauces that would dress up the blandest of pastas. Her creativity in the kitchen was a blessing to a family where money was tight and making new meals every day was a challenge.

Molly was also a gifted athlete as well as chef and secured a Lacrosse scholarship to Syracuse University. This was a blessing to her family as she was the first to go to college and at little cost to her parents. She took full advantage of her college education and earned a business degree. When she graduated, she joined her culinary skills and business acumen into a successful catering business. She wrote her first e-book after a customer asked if she could pay for several of her recipes. This sparked the entrepreneurial spirit in Mills and she thought if one person wanted them, then why not share the recipes with the world!

Molly lives near her family's home with her husband and three children and still cooks for her family every chance she gets. She plays Lacrosse with a local team made up of her old teammates from college and there are always some tasty nibbles on the ready after each game.

# Don't Miss Out!

Scan the QR-Code below and you can sign up to receive emails whenever Molly Mills publishes a new book. There's no charge and no obligation.

*Sign Me Up*

*https://molly.gr8.com*

Made in the USA
Coppell, TX
26 July 2022

80471921R00049